The Symbolism of the Tarot

Philosophy of Occultism in Pictures and Numbers

By

Peter Demianovitch Ouspensky

First published in 1913

Published by Left of Brain Books

Copyright © 2023 Left of Brain Books

ISBN 978-1-397-66925-4

First Edition

All rights reserved. No part of this publication may be reproduced, distributed, or transmitted in any form or by any means, including photocopying, recording, or other electronic or mechanical methods, without the prior written permission of the publisher, except in the case of brief quotations permitted by copyright law. Left of Brain Books is a division of Left Of Brain Onboarding Pty Ltd.

PUBLISHER'S PREFACE

About the Book

"An evocative inner journey through the Major Arcana of the Tarot."

(Quote from sacred-texts.com)

About the Author

Peter Demianovitch Ouspensky (1878 - 1947)

"Follower of early twentieth-century spiritual teacher Georgei I. Gurdjieff (1877-1949) and interpreter of his system. Ouspensky was born in Russia in 1878. He became a student of mathematics at Moscow University, then went on to become a journalist.

In 1907, motivated by the conviction that some higher form of knowledge must exist beyond the tangent fields of science and math, Ouspensky became aware of Theosophical literature and the possible synthesis of religion, mysticism, and science. In 1909, he published The Fourth Way, dealing with abstract mathematical concepts. He later published a book on yoga, followed by Tertium Organum; the Third Canon of Thought; a Key to the Enigmas of the World (English translation London, 1923). It offered his synthesis of time, space, relativity, Theosophy, cosmic consciousness, and Eastern and Western philosophy.

From 1913, Ouspensky traveled on an extended journey to Egypt, India, and Ceylon, searching for the miraculous, and upon his return gave a series of lectures on his experiences. In 1915, he met Sophia Grigorievna Maximenko (who later became his wife) and the mystic G. I. Gurdjieff (who became his guru).

Ouspensky became a disciple and interpreter of Gurdjieff's system (i.e., that there exists real possibilities for individuals to evolve psychologically into a state of consciousness far higher than that in which they spend the whole of their ordinary lives) until 1924, when he decided to follow his own path. He lectured, wrote books, and conducted study groups in England and the United States on the work of Gurdjieff until his death in 1947. Rom Landau attended and wrote an account of an Ouspensky lecture in London."

(Quote from answers.com)

CONTENTS

PUBLISHER'S PREFACE
WHAT IS THE TAROT? 1
THE SYMBOLS 17
    THE MAGICIAN 18
    THE FOOL... 20
    THE HIGH PRIESTESS 22
    THE WORLD 24
    THE EMPRESS 25
    JUDGMENT 27
    THE EMPEROR 28
    THE SUN 30
    THE CHARIOT.. 31
    THE MOON 33
    THE LOVERS 34
    THE STAR 36
    THE HIEROPHANT 39
    THE TOWER 41
    POWER 43
    THE DEVIL 44
    THE HERMIT 46
    TIME (TEMPERANCE).. 48
    THE WHEEL OF CHANCE 51
    DEATH 52
    JUSTICE 54
    THE HANGED MAN 55

WHAT IS THE TAROT?

NO study of occult philosophy is possible without an acquaintance with symbolism, for if the words occultism and symbolism are correctly used, they mean almost one and the same thing. Symbolism cannot be learned as one learns to build bridges or speak a foreign language, and for the interpretation of symbols a special cast of mind is necessary; in addition to knowledge, special faculties, the power of creative thought and a developed imagination are required. One who understands the use of symbolism in the arts, knows, in a general way, what is meant by occult symbolism. But even then a special training of the mind is necessary, in order to comprehend the "language of the Initiates", and to express in this language the intuitions as they arise.

There are many methods for developing the "sense of symbols" in those who are striving to understand the hidden forces of Nature and Man, and for teaching the fundamental principles as well as the elements of the esoteric language. The most synthetic, and one of the most interesting of these methods, is the Tarot In its exterior form the Tarot is a pack of cards used in the south of Europe for games and fortune-telling. These cards were first known in Europe at the end of the fourteenth century, when they were in use among the Spanish gypsies.

A pack of Tarot contains the fifty-two ordinary playing cards with the addition of one "picture card" to every suit, namely, the Knight, placed between the Queen and the Knave. These fifty-six cards are divided into four suits, two black and two red and have the following designation: sceptres (clubs), cups (hearts), swords (spades), and pentacles or disks (diamonds). In addition to the fifty-six cards the pack of Tarot has twenty-two numbered cards with special names:--

1. The Magician.	12. The Hanged Man.
2. The High Priestess.	13. Death.
3. The Empress.	14. Temperance.
4. The Emperor.	15. The Devil.
5. The Chariot. (7).	16. The Tower.
6. The Lovers.	17. The Star.
7. The Hierophant. (5).	18. The Moon.
8. Strength.	19. The Sun.
9. The Hermit.	20. Judgment.
10. The Wheel of Fortune.	21. The World.
11. Justice.	0. The Fool.

This pack of cards, in the opinion of many investigators, represents the Egyptian hieroglyphic book of seventy-eight tablets, which came to us almost miraculously.

The history of the Tarot is a great puzzle. During the Middle Ages, when it first appeared historically, there existed a tendency to build up synthetic symbolical or logical systems of the same sort as Ars Magna by Raymond Lully. But productions similar to the Tarot exist in India and China, so that we cannot possibly think it one of those systems created during the Middle Ages in Europe; it is also evidently connected with the Ancient Mysteries and the Egyptian Initiations. Although its origin is in oblivion and the aim of its author or authors quite unknown, there is no doubt whatever that it is the most complete code of Hermetic symbolism we possess.

Although represented as a pack of cards, the Tarot really is something quite different. It can be "read" in a variety of ways. As one instance, I shall give a metaphysical interpretation of the general meaning or of the general content of the book of Tarot, that is to say, its metaphysical title, which will plainly show that this work could not have been invented by illiterate gypsies of the fourteenth century.

The Tarot falls into three divisions: The first part has twenty-one numbered cards; the second part has one card 0; the third part has fifty-six cards, i. e., the four suits of fourteen cards. Moreover, the second part appears to be a link between the first and third parts, since all the fifty-six cards of the third part together are equal to the card 0.

Now, if we imagine twenty-one cards disposed in the shape of a triangle, seven cards on each side, a point in the centre of the triangle represented by the zero card, and a square round the triangle (the square consisting of fifty-six cards, fourteen on each side), we shall have a representation of the relation between God, Man and the Universe, or the relation between the world of ideas, the consciousness of man and the physical world.

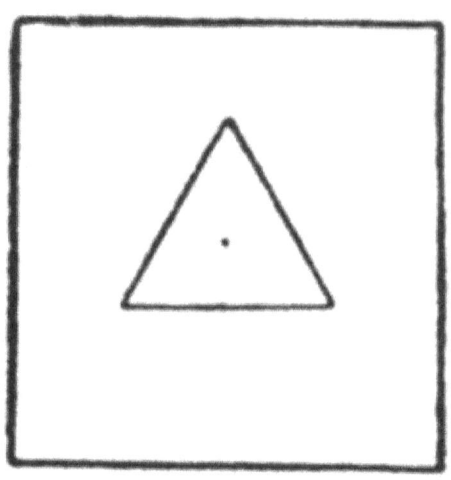

The triangle is God (the Trinity) or the world of ideas, or the noumenal world. The point is man's soul. The square is the visible, physical or phenomenal world. Potentially, the point is equal to the square, which means that all the visible world is contained in man's consciousness, is created in man's soul. And the soul itself is a point having no dimension in the world of the spirit, symbolized by the triangle. It is clear that such an idea could not have originated with ignorant people and clear also that the Tarot is something more than a pack of playing or fortune-telling cards.

H. P. Blavatsky mentions the Tarot in her works, and we have some reason for believing that she studied the Tarot. It is known that she loved to "play patience". We do not know what she read in the cards as she played this game, but the author was told that Madame Blavatsky searched persistently and for a long time for a MSS. on the Tarot.

In order to become acquainted with the Tarot, it is necessary to understand the basic ideas of the Kabala and of Alchemy. For it represents, as, indeed, many commentators of the Tarot think, a summary of the Hermetic Sciences--the Kabala, Alchemy, Astrology, Magic, with their different divisions. All these sciences, attributed to Hermes Trismegistus, really represent one system of a very broad and deep psychological investigation of the nature of man in his relation to the world of noumena (God, the world of Spirit) and to the world of phenomena (the visible, physical world). The letters of the Hebrew alphabet and the various allegories of the Kabala, the names of metals, acids and salts in alchemy; of planets and constellations in astrology; of good and evil spirits in magic--all these were only means to veil truth from the uninitiated.

But when the true alchemist spoke of seeking for gold, he spoke of gold in the soul of man. And he called gold that which in the New Testament is called the Kingdom of Heaven, and in Buddhism, Nirvana. And when the true astrologer spoke of constellations and planets he spoke of constellations and planets in the soul of man, i.e., of the qualities of the human soul and its relations to God and to the world. And when the true Kabalist spoke of the Name of God, he sought this Name in the soul of man and in Nature, not in dead books, nor in biblical texts, as did the Kabalist-Scholastics. The Kabala, Alchemy, Astrology, Magic are parallel symbolical systems of psychology and metaphysics. Any alchemical sentence may be read in a Kabalistic or astrological way, but the meaning will always be psychological and metaphysical.

We are surrounded by a wall built of our conceptions of the world, and are unable to look over this wall at the real world. The Kabala presents an effort to break this "enchanted circle". It investigates the world as it is, the world in itself.

The world in itself, as the Kabalists hold, consists of four elements, or the four principles forming One. These four principles are represented by the four letters of the name of Jehovah. The basic idea of the Kabala consists in the study of the Name of God in its manifestation. Jehovah in Hebrew is spelt by four letters, Yod, He, Vau and He--I. H. V. H. To these four letters is given the deepest symbolical meaning. The first letter expresses the active principle, the beginning or first cause, motion, energy, "I"; the second letter expresses the passive element, inertia, quietude, "not I;" the third, the balance of opposites, "form"; and the fourth, the result or latent energy.

The Kabalists affirm that every phenomenon and every object consists of these four principles, i.e., that every object and every phenomenon consists of the Name of God (The Word),--Logos.

The study of this Name (or the four-lettered word, tetragrammaton, in Greek) and the finding of it in everything constitutes the main problem of Kabalistic philosophy.

To state it in another way the Kabalists hold that these four principles penetrate and create everything. Therefore, when the man finds these four principles in things and phenomena of quite different categories (where before he had not seen similarity), he begins to see analogy between these phenomena. And, gradually, he becomes convinced that the whole world is built according to one and the same law, on one and the same plan. The richness and growth of his intellect consists in the widening of his faculty for finding analogies. Therefore the study of the law of the four letters, or the name of Jehovah presents a powerful means for widening consciousness.

This idea is perfectly clear, for if the Name of God be really in all (if God be present in all), all should be analogous to each other--the smallest particle analogous to the whole, the speck of dust analogous to the universe, and all analogous to God. The Name of God, the Word or Logos is the origin of the world. Logos also means Reason; the Word is the Logos, the Reason of everything.

There is a complete correspondence between the Kabala and Alchemy and Magic. In Alchemy the four elements which constitute the real world are called fire, water, air and earth; these fully correspond in significance with the four kabalistic letters. In Magic they are expressed as the four classes of spirits: elves (or salamanders), undines, sylphs and gnomes.

The Tarot in its turn is quite analogous to the Kabala, Alchemy and Magic, and, as it were, includes them. Corresponding to the four first principles or four letters of the Name of God, or the four alchemistic elements, or the four classes of spirits, the Tarot has four suits--sceptres, cups, swords and pentacles. Thus every suit, every side of the square, equal to the point, represents one of the elements, controls one class of spirits. The sceptres are fire or elves (or salamanders); the cups are water or undines; the swords are air or sylphes; and pentacles, earth or gnomes. Moreover, in every suit the King means the first principle or fire; the Queen--the second principle or water; the Knight--the third principle or air, and the Page (knave)--the fourth principle or earth.

Then again, the ace means fire; the deuce water; the three-spot, air; the four-spot earth. Then again the four-spot is the first principle, the five spot, the second etc.

In regard to the suits, one may add that the black suits (sceptres and swords) express activity and energy, will, initiative and the subjective side of consciousness; and the red (cups and pentacles) express passivity, inertia and the objective side of consciousness. Then the first two suits (sceptres and cups) signify "good" and the other two (swords and pentacles) mean "evil". Thus every card of the fifty-six indicates (independently of its number) the presence of the principle of activity or passivity, of "good" or "evil", arising either in man's will or from without. And the significance of each card is further deciphered thorough its various combinations with the suits and numbers in their symbolical meaning. The fifty-six cards as a whole represent, as it were, a complete picture of all the possibilities of man's consciousness. And this makes the Tarot adaptable for fortune-telling. Thus, including the Kabala, Astrology, Alchemy and Magic, the Tarot makes it possible to "seek gold", "to evoke spirits," and "to draw horoscopes", simply by means of this pack of cards without the complicated paraphernalia and ceremonies of an alchemist, astrologer or magician.

But the main interest of Tarot is in the twenty-two numbered cards. These cards have numerical meaning and also a very involved symbolical significance.

The literature relating to the Tarot has in view mainly the reading of the symbolical designs of the twenty-two cards. Very many writers on occultism have arranged their works on the plan of the Tarot. But this is not often suspected because the Tarot is rarely mentioned. Oswald Wirth speaks of origin of the Tarot in his Essay upon the Astronomical Tarot.

"According to Christian, [1] the twenty-two major arcana of the Tarot represent the hieroglyphic paintings which were found in the spaces between the columns of a gallery which the neophyte was obliged to cross in the Egyptian initiations. There

---

[1] "Histoire do la Magie".

were twelve columns to the north and the same number to the south, that is, eleven symbolical pictures on each side. These pictures were explained to the candidate for initiation in regular order, and they contained the rules and principles for the Initiate. This opinion is confirmed by the correspondence which exists between arcana when they are thus arranged."

In the gallery of the Temple the pictures were arranged in pairs, one opposite another, so that the last picture was opposite the first, the last but one opposite the second, etc. When the cards are so placed we find a highly interesting and deep suggestion. In this way the mind finds the one in the two, and is led from dualism to monism, which is what we might call the unification of the duad. One card explains the other and each pair shows moreover that they can be only mutually explanatory and mean nothing when taken separately.

Thus, for instance, the cards 10 and 13 ("Life" and "Death") signify together a certain whole or complementary condition which we cannot conceive by the ordinary, imperfect mental processes. We think of life and death as two "opposites", antagonistic one to the other, but, if we thought further, we should see that each depends on the other for existence and neither could come into existence separately.

A symbol may serve to transfer our intuitions and to suggest new ones only so long as its meaning is not defined. Real symbols are perpetually in process of creation; but when they receive a definite significance they become hieroglyphs and finally a mere alphabet. As this they express simply ordinary concepts, cease to be a language of the Gods or of initiates and become a language of men which everyone may learn.

Properly speaking, a symbol in occultism means the same as in art. If an artist uses ready-made symbols his work will not be true art, but only pseudo-art. If an occultist begins to use ready-made symbols, his work will not be truly occult, for it will contain no esotericism, no mysticism, but only pseudo-occultism, pseudo-esotericism, pseudo-mysticism. Symbolism in which the symbols have definite meanings is pseudo-symbolism.

Having made this idea clear in his mind, the author found that the key to the Tarot must lie in imagination and he decided to make an effort to re-design the cards, giving descriptive pictures of the Tarot, and to interpret the symbols, not by means of analysis, but by synthesis. The reader will find in the following little "pen pictures" reflections of many authors who wrote on the Tarot as St. Martin, Eliphas Levi, Dr. Papus etc. and of other authors who certainly never thought of the Tarot as, for example, Plotinus, Gichtel (XVII century), Friedrich Nietzsche, M. Collins etc., who came nevertheless to the same fundamental principles as the unknown authors of the Tarot.

Descriptions of the arcanas in these "pen pictures" often represent a conception which is almost entirely subjective, for instance, that of card 18. And the author likes to think that another might conceive of the same symbols differently, in any case he considers this quite possible.

Any one interested in this philosophical puzzle might well ask, What then is the Tarot? Is it a doctrine or merely a method? Is it a definite system or merely an alphabet by means of which any system may be constructed? In short, is it a book containing specific teachings, or is it merely an apparatus, a machine which we may use to build anything, even a new universe.

The author believes that the Tarot may be used for both purposes, though, of course, the contents of a book that may be read either forward or backward cannot be said to be, in the ordinary sense, strictly definite. But perhaps we find in this very indefiniteness of the Tarot and in the complexity of its philosophy, the element which constitutes its definiteness. The fact that we question the Tarot as to whether it be a method or a doctrine shows the limitation of our "three dimensional mind," which is unable to rise above the world of form and contra-positions or to free itself from thesis and antithesis! Yes, the Tarot contains and expresses any doctrine to be found in our consciousness, and in this sense it has definiteness. It represents Nature in all the richness of its infinite possibilities, and there is in it as in Nature, not one but all potential meanings. And these meanings are fluent and ever-changing, so the Tarot cannot be specifically this or that, for it ever moves and yet is ever the same.

In the following "pen-pictures" cards are taken in pairs:--I and 0; II and XXI; III and XX etc.--in each pair one card completing the sense of another and two making one.

Card I.--"The Magician".

"Man" Superman. The Initiate. The Occultist. Higher consciousness. Human Logos. The kabalistic "Adam Kadmon". Humanity. "Homo Sapiens".

Card II.--"The High Priestess".

Occultism. Esoterism. Mysticism. Theosophy. Initiation. Isis. Mystery.

Card III.--"The Empress".

Nature in its phenomenal aspect. The ever renewing and re-creating force of Nature. The objective reality.

Card IV.--"The Emperor".

Tetragrammaton. The law of four. Latent energy of Nature. Logos in the full aspect with all possibilities of the new Logos. Hermetic philosophy.

Card V.--"The Chariot".

"Man." The Imagination. Magic. Self-suggestion. Self deceit. Artificial means of attainment. Pseudo-occultism. Pseudo-theosophy.

Card VI.--"The Lovers".

"Man". Another aspect of the "Adam Kadmon", the "Perfect Man", "The divine androgyne". Love as the efforts of "Adam Kadmon" to find himself. The equilibrium of contraries. The unification of the duad, as the means of attaining the Light.

Card VII.--"The Hierophant".

Mysticism. Theosophy. Esoteric side of all religions.

Card VIII.--"Strength".

The Real Power. Strength of love. Strength of Union (Magic chain). Strength of the Infinite. Occultism. Esoterism. Theosophy.

Card IX.--"The Hermit".

"Man". The Path to the Initiation. Seeking for truth in the right way. Inner Knowledge. Inner Light. Inner Force. Theosophy. Occultism.

Card X.--"The Wheel of Chance".

The Wheel of Life. The life ever changing and ever remaining the same. The Circle of Time and the four elements. The idea of the circle.

Card XI. -"Justice".

Truth. Real Knowledge. Inner Truth. Occultism. Esoterism. Theosophy.

Card XII.--"The Hanged Man".

"Man". The Pain of the higher consciousness bound by the limitations of the body and mind. Superman in the separate man.

Card XIII.--"Death".

Another aspect of Life. Going away in order to come back at the same time. Completion of the circle.

Card XIV.--"Temperance". (Time).

The first attainment. The "Arcanum Magnum" of the occultists. The Fourth Dimension. Higher space. "Eternal Now".

Card XV.--"The Devil".

"Man". Weakness. Falsehood. The Fall of man into separateness, into hatred and into finiteness.

Card XVI.--"The Tower".

Sectarianism. Tower of Babel. Exoterism. Confusion of tongues. Fall of exoterism. The force of Nature re-establishing the truth distorted by men.

Card XVII.--"The Star".

The real aspect of the Astral World. That which maybe seen in extasy. The imagination of Nature. Real Knowledge. Occultism.

Card XVIII.--"The Moon".

The Astral World as it is seen by the artificial means of magic. "Psychic", "spiritistic" world. Dreads of the night. The real light from above and the false representation of that light from below. Pseudo-mysticism.

Card XIX.--"The Sun".

The Symbol and manifestation of the tetragrammaton. Creative power. Fire of life.

Card XX.--"Judgment".

The resurrection. Constant victory of life over death. Creative activity of nature in the death.

Card XXI.--"World".

Nature. The World as it is. Nature in its noumenal aspect. Esoteric side of nature. That which is made known in esoterism.

Inner reality of things. Human consciousness in the circle of time between the four elements.

Card 0.--"The Fool".

"Man." An ordinary man. A separate man. The uninitiate Lower consciousness. The end of a ray not knowing its relation to the centre.

The twenty-two cards may be divided into three divisions including each seven cards of similar meaning, the 22-nd card (No 21) as a duplicate (of the No 10) standing outside the triangle or forming a point in its centre.

The three sets of sevens belong: the first one to the Man, the second to the Nature and the third to the higher knowledge or to the Theosophy in the large sense of the word.

The First set of 7.

Cards: I--Magician; 0--The Fool; V--The Chariot; IX--The Hermit; VI--Lovers; XV--The Devil; XII--The Hanged Man.

The contents of these seven cards if taken in time picture seven degrees of the path of Man in his way to the Superman, or if taken in the Eternal Now picture seven faces of Man or seven I-s of man co-existing in him. This last meaning represents the inner sense of the secret doctrine of the Tarot in its relations to Man.

The second set of 7 (Nature) includes cards: III.--The Empress; X--Life; XIII--Death; XIV--Time; XVI--The Tower; XIX--The Sun; XX--Judgement.

The third set of 7 (Theosophy) includes cards: II--The High Priestess; IV--The Emperor; VIII--Strength; VII--The Hierophant; XI-Justice; XVII--The Star; XVIII--The Moon.

THE SYMBOLS

THE MAGICIAN

I Saw the Man.

HIS figure reached from earth to heaven and was clad in a purple mantle. He stood deep in foliage and flowers and his head, on which was the head-band of an initiate, seemed to disappear mysteriously in infinity.

Before him on a cube-shaped altar were four symbols of magic-- the sceptre, the cup, the sword and the pentacle.

His right hand pointed to heaven, his left to earth. Under his mantle he wore a white tunic girded with a serpent swallowing its tail.

His face was luminous and serene, and, when his eyes met mine, I felt that he saw most intimate recesses of my soul. I saw myself reflected in him as in a mirror and in his eyes I seemed to look upon myself.

And I heard a voice saying:

--"Look, this is the Great Magician!

With his hands he unites heaven and earth, and the four elements that form the world are controlled by him.

The four symbols before him are the four letters of the name of God, the signs of the four elements, fire, water, air, earth."

I trembled before the depth of the mysteries A touched... The words I heard seemed to be littered by the Great Magician himself, and it was as though he spoke in me.

I was in deep trepidation and at moment I felt there was nothing, before me except the blue sky; but within me a window opened through which I could see unearthly things. and hear unearthly words.

THE FOOL

And I saw another man.

TIRED and lame he dragged himself along the dusty road, across the deserted plain under the scorching rays of the sun. He glanced sidelong with foolish, staring eyes, a half smile, half leer on his face; he knew not where he went, but was absorbed in his chimerical dreams which ran constantly in the same circle. His fool's cap was put on wrong side front, his garments were torn in the back; a wild lynx with glowing eyes sprang upon him from behind a rock and buried her teeth in his flesh. He stumbled, nearly fell, but continued to drag himself along, all the time holding on his shoulder a bag containing useless things, which he, in his stupidity, carried wherever he went.

Before him a crevice crossed the road and a deep precipice awaited the foolish wanderer. Then a huge crocodile with open mouth crawled out of the precipice. And I heard the voice say:--

"Look! This is the same man."

I felt my head whirl.

"What has he in the bag?" I inquired, not knowing why I asked. And after a long silence the voice replied: "The four magic symbols, the sceptre, the cup, the sword and the pentacle. The fool always carries them, although he has long since forgotten what they mean. Nevertheless they belong to him, even though he does not know their use. The symbols have not lost their power, they retain it in themselves.

THE HIGH PRIESTESS

WHEN I lifted the first veil and entered the outer court of the Temple of Initiation, I saw in half darkness the figure of a woman sitting on a high throne between two pillars of the temple, one white, and one black. Mystery emanated from her and was about her. Sacred symbols shone on her green dress; on her head was a golden tiara surmounted by a two-horned moon; on her knees she held two crossed keys and an open book. Between the two pillars behind the woman hung another veil all embroidered with green leaves and fruit of pomegranate.

And a voice said:

"To enter the Temple one must lift the second veil and pass between the two pillars. And to pass thus, one must obtain possession of the keys, read the book and understand the symbols. Are you able to do this?"

"I would like to be able," I said.

Then the woman turned her face to me and looked into my eyes without speaking. And through me passed a thrill, mysterious and penetrating like a golden wave; tones vibrated in my brain, a flame was in my heart, and I understood that she spoke to me, saying without words:

"This is the Hall of Wisdom. No one can reveal it, no one can hide it. Like a flower it must grow and bloom in thy soul. If thou wouldst plant the seed of this flower in thy soul--learn to discern the real from the false. Listen only to the Voice that is soundless... Look only on that which is invisible, and remember that in thee thyself, is the Temple and the gate to it, and the mystery, and the initiation."

THE WORLD

AN unexpected vision appeared to me. A circle not unlike a wreath woven from rainbow and lightnings, whirled from heaven to earth with a stupendous, velocity, blinding me by its brilliance. And amidst this light and fire I heard music and soft singing, thunderclaps and the roar of a tempest, the rumble of falling mountains and earthquakes.

The circle whirled with a terrifying noise, touching the sun and the earth, and, in the centre of it I saw the naked, dancing figure of a beautiful young woman, enveloped by a light, transparent scarf, in her hand she held a magic wand.

Presently the four apocalyptical beasts began to appear on the edges of the circle; one with the face of a lion, another with the face of a man, the third, of an eagle and the fourth, of a bull.

The vision disappeared as suddenly as it appeared. A weird silence fell on me. "What does it mean?" I asked in wonder.

"It is the image of the world," the voice said, "but it can be understood only after the Temple has been entered. This is a vision of the world in the circle of Time, amidst the four principles. But thou seest differently because thou seest the world outside thyself. Learn to see it in thyself and thou wilt understand the infinite essence, hidden in all illusory forms. Understand that the world which thou knowest is only one of the aspects of the infinite world, and things and phenomena are merely hierolgyphics of deeper ideas."

THE EMPRESS

I felt the breath of the spring, and accompanying the fragrance of violets and lilies-of-the-valley I heard the tender singing of elves. Rivulets murmured, the treetops rustled, the grasses whispered, innumerable birds sang in choruses and bees hummed; everywhere I felt the breathing of joyful, living Nature.

The sun shone tenderly and softly and a little white cloud hung over the woods.

In the midst of a green meadow where primroses bloomed, I saw the Empress seated on a throne covered with ivy and lilacs. A green wreath adorned her golden hair and, above her head, shone twelve stars. Behind her rose two snowy wings and in her hands she held a sceptre. All around, beneath the sweet smile of the Empress, flowers and buds opened their dewy, green leaves. Her whole dress was covered with them as though each newly opened flower were reflected in it or had engraved itself thereon and thus become part of her garment.

The sign of Venus, the goddess of love, was chiselled on her marble throne.

"Queen of life," I said, "why is it so bright and joyful all about you? Do you not know of the grey, weary autumn, of the cold, white winter? Do you not know of death and graveyards with black graves, damp and cold? How can you smile so joyfully on the opening flowers, when everything is destined to death, even that which has not yet been born?"

For answer the Empress looked on me still smiling and, under the influence of that smile, I suddenly felt a flower of some clear understanding open in my heart.

JUDGMENT

I saw an ice plain, and on the horizon, a chain of snowy mountains. A cloud appeared and began to grow until it covered a quarter of the sky. Two fiery wings suddenly expanded in the cloud, and I knew that I beheld the messenger of the Empress.

He raised a trumpet and blew through it vibrant, powerful tones. The plain quivered in response to him and the mountains loudly rolled their echoes. One after another, graves opened in the plain and out of them came men and women, old and young, and children. They stretched out their arms toward the Messenger of the Empress and to catch the sounds of his trumpet.

And in its tones I felt the smile of the Empress and in the opening graves I saw the opening flowers whose fragrance seemed to be wafted by the outstretched arms.

Then I understood the mystery of birth in death.

THE EMPEROR

AFTER I learned the first three numbers I was given to understand the Great Law of Four--the alpha and omega of all.

I saw the Emperor on a lofty stone throne, ornamented by four rams' heads. On his forehead shone a golden helmet. His white beard fell over a purple mantle. In one hand he held a sphere, the symbol of his possession, and in the other, a sceptre in the form of an Egyptian cross--the sign of his power over birth.

"I am The Great Law," the Emperor said. "I am the name of God. The four letters of his name are in me and I am in all.

"I am in the four principles. I am in the four elements. I am in the four seasons. I am in the four cardinal points. I am in the four signs of the Tarot.

"I am the beginning; I am action; I am completion; I am the result.

"For him who knows how to see me there are no mysteries on earth.

"I am the great Pentacle.

"As the earth encloses in itself fire, water and air; as the fourth letter of the Name encloses in itself the first three and becomes itself the first, so my sceptre encloses the complete triangle and bears in itself the seed of a new triangle.

"I am the Logos in the full aspect and the beginning of a new Logos."

And while the Emperor spoke, his helmet shone brighter and brighter, and his golden armour gleamed beneath his mantle. I could not bear his glory and I lowered my eyes.

When I tried to lift them again a vivid light of radiant fire was before me, and I prostrated myself and made obeisance to the Fiery Word.

THE SUN

AS soon as I perceived the Sun, I understood that It, Itself, is the expression of the Fiery Word and the sign of the Emperor.

The great luminary shone with an intense heat upon the large golden heads of sun-flowers.

And I saw a naked boy, whose head was wreathed with roses, galloping on a white horse and waving a bright-red banner.

I shut my eyes for a moment and when I opened them again I saw that each ray of the Sun is the sceptre of the Emperor and bears life. And I saw how under the concentration of these rays the mystic flowers of the waters open and receive the rays into themselves and how all Nature is constantly born from the union of two principles.

THE CHARIOT

I saw a chariot drawn by two sphinxes, one white, the other black. Four pillars supported a blue canopy, on which were scattered five-pointed stars. The Conqueror, clad in steel armour, stood under this canopy guiding the sphinxes. He held a sceptre, on the end of which were a globe, a triangle and a square. A golden pentagram sparkled in his crown. On the front of the chariot there was represented a winged sphere and beneath that the symbol of the mystical lingam, signifying the union of two principles.

"Everything in this picture has a significance. Look and try to understand", said the voice.

"This is Will armed with Knowledge. We see here, however, the wish to achieve, rather than achievement itself. The man in the chariot thought himself a conqueror before he had really conquered, and he believes that victory must come to the conqueror. There are true possibilities in this beautiful conception, but also many false ones. Illusory fires and numerous dangers are hidden here.

He controls the sphinxes by the power of a magic word, but the tension of his Will may fail and then the magic word will lose its power and he may be devoured by the sphinxes.

This is indeed the Conqueror, but only for the moment; he has not yet conquered Time, and the succeeding moment is unknown to him.

This is the Conqueror, not by love, but by fire and the sword,--a conqueror against whom the conquered may arise. Do you see behind him the towers of the conquered city? Perhaps the flame of uprising burns already there.

And he is unaware that the city vanquished by means of fire and the sword is the city within his own consciousness, that the magic chariot is in himself and that the blood-thirsty sphynxes, also a state of consciousness within, watch his every movement. He has externalized all these phases of his mind and sees them only outside himself. This is his fundamental error. He entered the outer court of the Temple of knowledge, but thinks he has been in the Temple itself. He regarded the rituals of the first tests as initiation, and he mistook for the goddess, the priestess who guarded the threshold. Because of this misconception great perils await him.

Nevertheless it may be that even in his errors and perils the Great Conception lies concealed. He seeks to know and, perhaps, in order to attain, mistakes, dangers and even failures are necessary.

Understand that this is the same man whom you saw uniting Heaven and Earth, and again walking across a hot desert to a precipice.

THE MOON

A desolate plain stretched before me. A full moon looked down as if in contemplative hesitation. Under her wavering light the shadows lived their own peculiar life. On the horizon I saw blue hills, and over them wound a path which stretched between two grey towers far away into the distance. On either side the path a wolf and dog sat and howled at the moon. I remembered that dogs believe in thieves and ghosts. A large black crab crawled out of the rivulet into the sands. A heavy, cold dew was falling.

Dread fell upon me. I sensed the presence of a mysterious world, a world of hostile spirits, of corpses rising from graves, of wailing ghosts. In this pale moonlight I seemed to feel the presence of apparitions; someone watched me from behind the towers,--and I knew it was dangerous to look back.

THE LOVERS

I saw a blooming garden in a green valley, surrounded by soft blue hills.

In the garden I saw a Man and a Woman naked and beautiful. They loved each other and their Love was their service to the Great Conception, a prayer and a sacrifice; through It they communed with God, through It they received the highest revelations; in Its light the deepest truths came to them; the magic world opened its gate; elves, undines, sylphs and gnomes came openly to them; the three kingdoms of nature, the mineral, plant and animal, and the four elements--fire, water, air and earth-served them.

Through their Love they saw the mystery of the world's equilibrium, and that they themselves were a symbol and expression of this balance. Two triangles united in them into a six-pointed star. Two magnets melted into an ellipsis. They were two. The third was the Unknown Future. The three made One.

I saw the woman looking out upon the world as though enraptured with its beauty. And from the tree on which ripened golden fruit I saw a serpent creep It whispered in the woman's ear, and I saw her listening, smiling at first suspiciously, then with curiosity which merged into joy. Then I saw her speak to the man. I noticed that he seemed to admire only her and smiled with an expression of joy and sympathy at all she told him.

"This picture you see, is a picture of temptation and fall", said the voice. "What constitutes the Fall? Do you understand its nature"?

"Life is so good", I said, "and the world so beautiful, and this man and woman wanted to believe in the reality of the world and of themselves. They wanted to forget service and take from the world what it can give. So they made a distinction between themselves and the world. They said, 'We are here, the world is there'. And the world separated from them and became hostile."

"Yes", said the Voice, this is true. "The everlasting mistake with men is that they see the fall in love. But Love is not a fall, it is a soaring above an abyss. And the higher the flight, the more beautiful and alluring appears the earth. But that wisdom, which crawls on earth, advises belief in the earth and in the present. This is the Temptation. And the man and woman yielded to it. They dropped from the eternal realms and submitted to time and death. The balance was disturbed. The fairyland was closed upon them. The elves, undines, sylphs and gnomes became invisible.

The Face of God ceased to reveal Itself to them, and all things appeared upside down.

"This Fall, this first 'sin of man', repeats itself perpetually, because man continues to believe in his separateness and in the Present. And only by means of great suffering can he liberate himself from the control of time and return to Eternity--leave darkness and return to Light".

THE STAR

A strange emotion seized me. A fiery trembling ran in waves through all my body. My heart quickened its beating, tumult agitated my mind.

I felt that I was surrounded by portentous mysteries. And presently shafts of Light penetrated my being and illuminated many things before in darkness, whose existence even I had never suspected. Veils vanished of which I had been before unaware. Voices spoke to me. And suddenly all my former knowledge took a new and different meaning.

I discovered unexpected correlations in things which hitherto I had thought foreign to each other. Objects distant and different from one another appeared near and similar. The facts of the world arranged themselves before my eyes according to a new pattern.

In the sky there appeared an enormous star surrounded by seven smaller stars. Their rays intermingled, filling space with immeasurable radiance and splendour. Then I knew I saw that Heaven of which Plotinus speaks:

"Where . . . all things are diaphanous; and nothing is dark and resisting, but everything is apparent to every one internally and throughout. For light everywhere meets with light, since everything contains all things in itself, and again sees all things in another. So that all things are everywhere, and all is all. Each thing likewise is everything. And the splendour there is infinite.

For everything there is great, since even that which is small is great.

"The sun too, which is there, is all the stars; and again each star is the sun and all the stars. In each however, a different property predominates, but at the same time all things are visible in each. Motion likewise there is pure; for motion is not confounded by a mover different from it. Permanency also suffers no change of its nature, because it is not mingled with the unstable. And the beautiful there is beautiful, because it does not subsist in beauty. Each thing, too, is there established, not as in a foreign land, but the seat of each thing is that which each thing is. . . . . Nor is the thing itself different from the place in which it subsists. For the subject of it is intellect, and it is itself intellect. . . . In this sensible region, therefore, one part is not produced by another, but each part is alone a part. But there each part always proceeds from the whole, and is at the same each time part and the whole. For it appears indeed as a part; but by him whose sight is acute, it will be seen as a whole.

"Where . . . is likewise no weariness of the vision which Is there, not any plenitude of perception which can bring intuition to an end.

"For neither was there any vacuity which when filled might cause the visible energy to cease; nor is this one thing, but that another, so as to occasion a part of one thing not to be amicable with that of another.

"Where . . . the life is wisdom; a wisdom not obtained by a reasoning process, because the whole of it always was, and is not in any respect deficient, so as to be in want of investigation. But it is the first wisdom, and is not derived from another".

I understood that all the radiance here is thought; and the changing colours are emotions. And each ray, if we look into it, turns into images, symbols, voices and moods. And I saw that there is nothing inanimate, but all is soul, all is life, all is emotion and imagination.

And beneath the radiant stars beside the blue river I saw a naked maiden, young and beautiful. She stooped on one knee and poured water from two vessels, one of gold and one of silver. A little bird in a near by bush lifted its wings and was poised ready to fly away.

For a moment I understood that I beheld the Soul of Nature.

"This is Nature's Imagination," said the voice gently. "Nature dreams, improvises, creates worlds. Learn to unite your imagination with Her Imagination and nothing will ever be impossible for you. Lose the external world and seek it in yourself. Then you will find Light. "But remember, unless you have lost the Earth, you will not find Heaven. It is impossible to see both wrongly and rightly at the same time."

THE HIEROPHANT

I saw the great Master in the Temple. He was siting on a golden throne set upon a purple platform, and he wore the robe of a high priest with a golden tiara. He held a golden eight-pointed cross, and lying at his feet were two crossed keys. Two initiates bowed before him and to them he spoke:--

"Seek the Path, do not seek attainment, Seek for the Path within yourself.

"Do not expect to hear the truth from others, nor to see it, or read it in books. Look for the truth in yourself, not without yourself.

"Aspire only after the impossible and inaccessible. Expect only that which shall not be.

"Do not hope for Me,--do not look for Me,--do not believe--that I am outside yourself.

"Within your soul build a lefty tower by which you may ascend to Heaven. Do not believe in external miracles, expect miracles only within you. Beware of believing in a mystery of the earth, in a mystery guarded by men; for treasuries which must be guarded are empty. Do not search for a mystery that can be hidden by men. Seek the Mystery within yourself.

"Above all, avoid those towers built in order to preserve the mysteries and to make an ascent to Heaven by stone stairways.

And remember that as soon as men build such a tower they begin to dispute about the summit.

"The Path is in yourself, and Truth is in yourself and Mystery is in yourself."

THE TOWER

I saw a lofty tower extending from earth to heaven; its golden crowned summit reached beyond the clouds. All round it black night reigned and thunder rumbled.

Suddenly the heavens opened, a thunder-clap shook the whole earth, and lightning struck the summit of the tower and felled the golden crown. A tongue of fire shot from heaven and the whole tower became filled with fire and smoke. Then I beheld the builders of the tower fall headlong to the ground.

And the voice said:--

"The building of the tower was begun by the disciples of the great Master in order to have a constant reminder of the Master's teaching that the true tower must be built in one's own soul, that in the tower built by hands there can be no mysteries, that no one can ascend to Heaven by treading stone steps.

"The tower should warn the people not to believe in it. It should serve as a reminder of the inner Temple and as a protection against the outer; it should be as a lighthouse, in a dangerous place where men have often been wrecked and where ships should not go.

"But by and by the disciples forgot the true covenant of the Master and what the tower symbolized, and began to believe in the tower of stone, they had built, and to teach others to so believe. They began to say that in this tower there is power, mystery and the spirit of the Master, that the tower itself is holy and that it is built for the coming Master according to His covenant and His will. And so they waited in the tower for the Master. Others did not believe this, or interpreted it differently. Then began disputes about the rights of the summit. Quarrels started, 'Our Master, your Master,' was said; 'our tower, your tower.' And the disciples ceased to understand each other. Their tongues had become confused.

"You understand the meaning here? They had begun to think that this is the tower of the Master, that He builds it through them, and that it must and, indeed, can be built right up to Heaven.

"And you see how Heaven responded?"

POWER

IN the midst of a green plain, surrounded by blue hills, I saw a woman with a lion. Girdled with wreaths of roses, a symbol of infinity over her head, the woman calmly and confidently covered the lion's mouth and the lion obediently licked her hand.

"This is a picture of power", said the voice. "It has different meanings. First it shows the power of love. Love alone can conquer wrath. Hatred feeds hatred. Remember what Zarathustra said: "Let man be freed from vengeance; this is a bridge for me which leads to higher hope and a rainbow in heaven after long storms".

"Then it shows power of unity. These wreaths of roses suggest a magic chain. Unity of desires, unity of aspirations creates such power that every wild, uncontrolled, unconscious force is subdued. Even two desires, if united, are able to conquer almost the whole world.

"The picture also shows the power of infinity, that sphere of mysteries. For a consciousness that perceives the symbol of infinity above it, knows no obstacles and cannot be withstood".

THE DEVIL

BLACK, awful night enveloped the earth. An ominous, red flame burned in the distance. I was approaching a fantastic figure which outlined itself before me as I came nearer to it. High above the earth appeared the repulsive red face of the Devil, with large, hairy ears, pointed beard and curved goats' horns. A pentagram, pointing downwards, shone in phosphoric light between the horns on his forehead. Two large, grey, bat-like wings were spread behind him. He held up one arm, spreading out his bare, fat hand. In the palm I saw the sign of black magic. A burning torch held down-end in his other hand emitted black, stifling smoke. He sat on a large, black cube, gripping it with the claws of his beast-like, shaggy legs.

A man and woman were chained to the cube--the same Man and Woman I saw in the garden, but now they had horns and tails tipped with flame. And they were evidently dissatisfied in spirit, and were filled with protest and repulsion.

"This is a picture of weakness", said the voice, "a picture of falsehood and evil. They are the same man and woman you saw in the garden, but their love ceasing to be a sacrifice, became an illusion. This man and woman forgot that their love is a link in the chain that unites them with eternity, that their love is a symbol of equilibrium and a road to Infinity.

"They forgot that It is a key to the gate of the magic world, the torch which lights the higher Path. They forgot that Love is real and immortal and they subjugated it to the unreal and temporary. And they each made love a tool for submitting the other to himself.

"Then love became dissension and fettered them with iron chains to the black cube of matter, on which sits deceit".

And I heard the voice of the Devil: "I am Evil", he said, "at least so far as Evil can exist in this best of worlds. In order to see me, one must be able to see unfairly, incorrectly and narrowly. I close the triangle, the other two sides of which are Death and Time. In order to quit this triangle it is necessary to see that it does not exist.

"But how to do this is not for me to tell. For I am the Evil which men say is the cause of all evil and which they invented as an excuse for all the evil that they do.

"They call me the Prince of Falsehood, and truly I am the prince of lies, because I am the most monstrous production of human lies".

THE HERMIT

AFTER long wanderings over a sandy, waterless desert where only serpents lived, I met the Hermit.

He was wrapped in a long cloak, a hood thrown over his head. He held a long staff in one hand and in the other a lighted lantern, though it was broad daylight and the sun was shining.

"The lantern of Hermes Trismegistus", said the voice, "this is higher knowledge, that inner knowledge which illuminates in a new way even what appears to be already clearly known. This lantern lights up the past, the present and the future for the Hermit, and opens the souls of people and the most intimate recesses. of their hearts."

"The cloak of Apollonius is the faculty of the wise man by which he isolates himself, even amidst a noisy crowd; it is his skill in hiding his mysteries, even while expressing them, his capacity for silence and his power to act in stillness.

"The staff of the patriarchs is his inner authority, his power, his self-confidence."

The lantern, the cloak and the staff are the three symbols of initiation. They are needed to guide souls past the temptation of illusory fires by the roadside, so that they may go straight to the higher goal. He who receives these three symbols or aspires to obtain them, "strives to enrich himself with all he can acquire, not for himself, but, like God, to delight in the joy of giving".

"The giving virtue is the basis of an initiate's life.

"His soul is transformed into 'a spoiler of all treasures' so said Zarathustra.

"Initiation unites the human mind with the higher mind by a chain of analogies. This chain is the ladder leading to heaven, dreamed of by the patriarch".

TIME (TEMPERANCE)

AN angel in a white robe, touching earth and heaven, appeared. His wings were flame and a radiance of gold was about his head. On his breast he wore the sacred sign of the book of the Tarot-- a triangle within a square, a point within the triangle; on his forehead the symbol of life and eternity, the circle.

In one hand was a cup of silver, in the other a cup of gold and there flowed between these cups a constant, glistening stream of every colour of the rainbow. But I could not tell from which cup nor into which cup the stream flowed.

In great awe I understood that I was near the ultimate mysteries from which there is no return. I looked upon the angel, upon his symbols, his cups, the rainbow stream between the cups,--and my human heart trembled with fear and my human mind shrank with anguish and lack of understanding.

"Yes", said the voice, "this is a mystery that is revealed at Initiation. 'Initiation' is simply the revealing of this mystery in the soul. The Hermit receives the lantern, the cloak and the staff so that he can bear the light of this mystery.

"But you probably came here unprepared. Look then and listen and try to understand, for now understanding is your only salvation. He who approaches the mystery without complete comprehension will be lost.

"The name of the angel is Time. The circle on his forehead is the symbol of eternity and life. Each life is a circle which returns to the same point where it began. Death is the return to birth. And from one point to another on the circumference of a circle the distance is always the same, and the further it is from one point, the nearer it will be to the other.

"Eternity is a serpent, pursuing its tail, never catching it.

"One of the cups the angel holds is the past, the other is the future. The rainbow stream between the cups is the present. You see that it flows both ways.

"This is Time in its most incomprehensible aspect.

"Men think that all flows constantly in one direction. They do not see that everything perpetually meets and that Time is a multitude of turning circles. Understand this mystery and learn to discern the contrary currents in the rainbow stream of the present.

"The symbol of the sacred book of the Tarot on the angel's breast is the symbol of the correlation of God, Man and the Universe.

"The triangle is God, the world of spirit, the world of ideas. The point within the triangle is the soul of man. The square is the visible world.

"The consciousness of man is the spark of divinity, a point within the triangle of spirit. Therefore the whole square of the visible universe is equal to the point within the triangle.

"The world of spirit is the triangle of the twenty-one signs of the Tarot. The square represents fire, air, water and earth, and thus symbolises the world.

"All this, in the form of the four symbols, is in the bag of the Fool, who himself is a point in a triangle. Therefore a point without dimension contains an infinite square".

THE WHEEL OF CHANCE

I walked along, absorbed in deep thought, trying to understand the vision of the Angel. And suddenly, as I lifted my head, I saw midway in the sky a huge, revolving circle covered with Kabalistic letters and symbols. The circle turned with terrible velocity, and around it, falling down and flying up, symbolic figures of the serpent and the dog revolved; above it sat an immovable sphinx.

In clouds, on the four quarters of heaven, I saw the four apocalyptical beings, one with the face of a lion, another with the face of a bull, the third with a face of an eagle, and the fourth with the face of a bull. And each of them read an open book.

And I heard the voices of Zarathustra's beasts:--

"All go, all return,"--the wheel of life ever turns. All die, all flourish again,--the year of existence runs eternally.

"All perish, all live again, the same house of existence is ever building. All separate, all meet again, the ring of existence is ever true to itself.

"Existence begins at every moment. Round each "here" rolls "there". The middle is everywhere. The way of eternity is a curve".

DEATH

FATIGUED by the flashing of the Wheel of Life, I sank to earth and shut my eyes. But it seemed to me that the Wheel kept turning before me and that the four creatures continued sitting in the clouds and reading their books.

Suddenly, on opening my eyes, I saw a gigantic rider on a white horse, dressed in black armour, with a black helmet and black plume. A skeleton's face looked out from under the helmet. One bony hand held a large, black, slowly-waving banner, and the other held a black bridle ornamented with skulls and bones.

And, wherever the white horse passed, night and death followed; flowers withered, leaves drooped, the earth covered itself with a white shroud; graveyards appeared; towers, castles and cities were destroyed.

Kings in the full splendour of their fame and their power; beautiful women loved and loving; high priests invested by power from God; innocent children--when they saw the white horse all fell on their knees before him, stretched out their hands in terror and despair, and fell down to rise no more.

Afar, behind two towers, the sun sank.

A deadly cold enveloped me. The heavy hoofs of the horse seemed to step on my breast, and I felt the world sink into an abyss.

But all at once something familiar, but faintly seen and heard, seemed to come from the measured step of the horse. A moment more and I heard in his steps the movement of the Wheel of Life!

An illumination entered me, and, looking at the receding rider and the descending sun, I understood that the Path of Life consists of the steps of the horse of Death.

The sun sinks at one point and rises at another. Each moment of its motion is a descent at one point and an ascent at another. I understood that it rises while sinking and sinks while rising, and that life, in coming to birth, dies, and in dying, comes to birth.

"Yes," said the voice. The sun does not think of its going down and coming up. What does it know of earth, of the going and coming observed by men? It goes its own way, over its own orbit, round an unknown Centre. Life, death, rising and falling-- do you not know that all these things are thoughts and dreams and fears of the Fool"?

JUSTICE

WHEN I possessed the keys, read the book and understood the symbols, I was permitted to lift the curtain of the Temple and enter. its inner sanctum. And there I beheld a Woman with a crown of gold and a purple mantle. She held a sword in one hand and scales in the other. I trembled with awe at her appearance, which was deep and mysterious, and drew me like an abyss.

"You see Truth," said the voice. "On these scales everything is weighed. This sword is always raised to guard justice, and nothing can escape it.

"But why do you avert your eyes from the scales and the sword? They will remove the last illusions. How could you live on earth without these illusions?

"You wished to see Truth and now you behold it! But remember what happens to the mortal who beholds a Goddess!"

THE HANGED MAN

AND then I saw a man in terrible suffering, hung by one leg, head downward, to a high tree. And I heard the voice:--

"Look! This is a man who saw Truth. Suffering awaits the man on earth, who finds the way to eternity and to the understanding of the Endless.

"He is still a man, but he already knows much of what is inaccessible even to Gods. And the incommensurableness of the small and the great in his soul constitutes his pain and his golgotha.

"In his own soul appears the gallows on which he hangs in suffering, feeling that he is indeed inverted.

"He chose this way himself.

"For this he went over a long road from trial to trial, from initiation to initiation, through failures and falls.

"And now he has found Truth and knows himself.

"He knows that it is he who stands before an altar with magic symbols, and reaches from earth to heaven; that he also walks on a dusty road under a scorching sun to a precipice where a crocodile awaits him; that he dwells with his mate in paradise under the shadow of a blessing genius; that he is chained to a black cube under the shadow of deceit; that he stands as a victor for a moment in an illusionary chariot drawn by sphinxes; and that with a lantern in bright sunshine, he seeks for Truth in a desert.

"Now he has found Her".

www.ingramcontent.com/pod-product-compliance
Lightning Source LLC
Chambersburg PA
CBHW051607010526
44119CB00056B/808